Short Stories

from

Devayana

Third Epic of India

Short Stories

from

Devayana

Third Epic of India

Amita Nathwani
Maggie Voysey Paun

MOONLIGHT BOOKS

Short Stories from Devayana

FIRST EDITION: 2018

ISBN PB: 978-81-936313-7-9
ISBN EBOOK: 978-81-936313-8-6

Published by
MOONLIGHT BOOKS
20 Ekjot Apartment, Pitampura, Delhi-110034, India
Email: moonlightbooks2016@gmail.com
www.moonlightbooks.in

Printed by Replika Press Pvt. Ltd., India

Contents

Introduction

The stories in this book are taken from the Devayana, the third and little known epic of India which was written down by Dr Hajari, a young follower of the famous Yogi, Sri Aurobindo. It tells the story of the Four Ages of Time: the Treta Yuga (Silver Age), Dwapara Yuga (Bronze), Kali Yuga (Iron, in which we live) and the Satya Yuga or Golden Age.

The epic consists of more than twelve thousand pages of poetry divided into twelve volumes. First written in Bengali, it has been transcribed into Hindi/Sanskrit by Amita Nathwani, whose mother Dr Indira Sardana was a devotee in the Aurobindo Ashram in Pondicherry on the eastern coast of India. She had a serious heart condition which was healed by Dr Hajari, a homeopathic doctor, and when she learnt of the Devayana she determined to make its revelations known to a wider world.

This is how they were made known to Dr Hajari.

The night was dark. The air was still. Even the usually restless ocean seemed asleep. It was the spring of 1951 when the world was still bruised and shocked by a terrible war. New weapons had been discovered, whole cities destroyed. Millions of people had died. Yet countries that had fought together had now turned against each other and it seemed that the world was in danger of complete destruction.

From high above the earth at the very edge of the universe, Lord Shiva in the form of Pingal Maheshwara, the Divine Poet, met with Sri Aurobindo who had left this mortal world, the year before.

'Oh great Lord, must the battle between good and evil be never-ending?' asked Sri Aurobindo.

'Yes,' came Shiva's deep and powerful voice. 'But for once I think I must intervene and tip the balance in favour of the good. I shall send a message to the world, a new epic, and you may help me.'

'Only tell me how,' Sri Aurobindo replied.

'I need a human messenger,' the great God explained. 'Someone with deep faith and belief in the Gods and the ancient truths of the Vedas.'

'We can look in the Ashram where I was honoured and loved by many as a Guru,' Sri Aurobindo suggested. 'There are many good devotees there from whom you may choose.'

It was two o'clock in the morning and all the ashramites were asleep.

'OM,' chanted the God and the guru. 'OMMM. OMMMMM...'

But even the eternal sound of the universe was not enough to waken the sleepers. Sri Aurobindo was very disappointed but Lord Shiva comforted him.

'Once when I was here on a visit to you, I saw a young man sitting in deep meditation on the roof,' he said. 'I entered into his mind for a moment but even my great force did not distract him. Call on him.'

'OMMMMM,' chanted the guru again.

The young man, Dr Hajari, was also asleep but at the sound of his beloved guru's voice he awoke.

'My son, the great Lord Shiva himself has chosen you to be his messenger.'

Dr Hajari saw what seemed like a star exploding all around him and in the middle of this blinding light appeared the blazing figure of Shiva. Dr Hajari was overcome.

'I am not strong enough alone,' he told Sri Aurobindo. 'But stay with me in my mind and you may use my body as you wish.'

Lord Shiva knew that Sri Aurobindo had developed great powers during his long years of meditation and prayer. 'Let it be so,' he agreed.

Sri Aurobindo kissed his young disciple on the forehead and Dr Hajari felt a great happiness cascade like a waterfall down his face. The energy of a thousand lights flowed through his body and gave him the power to do as Lord Shiva wished.

But Sri Aurobindo still feared that the task would be too great and take too long for one man to complete. 'Human life is short,' he reminded the God. 'Can you not give your messenger more help?'

So Shiva called on Ganesh, the elephant-headed God, who is known as the Remover of Obstacles, to whom humans pray when they have some difficult task to accomplish. Ganesh came and Dr Hajari was filled with joy to find himself in such company.

From that moment he began to write down the divine words as they came to him from above. Every night he wrote ten pages and in only three years and four months, by the middle of July 1954, the great epic was complete.

☆☆☆☆☆

The Fight Between Indra and Vritra

In the beginning the Gods and demons lived in peace with their father the Creator and their two mothers Aditi and Diti. Aditi, the power of good, and Diti, the source of dark energy, worked in the constant creative cycles of the universe.

But slowly the young Gods and demons became restless and started to quarrel. Small arguments blew up into ugly fights and instead of being friendly they began to hate each other. Soon they could not bear to be near each other and wanted their own space where they could use their powers as they pleased.

Vritra, the oldest demon, and Indra, the oldest God, went together to ask their father what to do.

'What areas shall belong to us?' asked Indra.

'And what shall be our powers there?' asked Vritra.

'I am the Creator,' replied their father. 'The whole universe is mine. For you to know what powers you should have you must ask your mothers. What belongs to your mothers belongs to you.'

Indra asked Aditi. 'Mother, what is our area of influence in this Creation? And what are our duties?'

Aditi answered. 'It is simple. All of it belongs to your father and your duty is to do what pleases him.'

Vritra asked Diti the same question but she replied: 'Where I live belongs to me and as my children you must please me.'

Again Vritra went to his father. 'Who is right?' he asked. 'Do all the areas belong to you or, where my mother is, is that mine?'

Everyone gathered to hear how their father would solve the problem.

'There are seven heavens in my Creation,' he said. 'To attain each you must do many *yajnas,* make many sacrifices. The first heaven you may reach when you have completed ten *yajnas*, the second twenty and so on. And for the seventh, the very highest, you must carry out one hundred.'

Of course, both the Gods and the demons wanted to gain the seventh heaven.

Each *yajna* took at least one hundred years to perform and after nine thousand years when Indra had carried out ninety *yajnas*, he heard that Vritra had carried out ninety one.

'We cannot allow the demons to gain the seventh heaven,' he said to the other Gods. 'Somehow we must stop them.'

In secret, he went to the place where the demons were holding their *yajnas*. He saw there a huge mound of ghee which they needed to carry out the remaining nine *yajnas*, and he stole it all. And so the Gods won the right to live in and look after the seventh heaven.

Of course, Vritra was very angry and he declared war on the Gods. There was a terrible battle which raged on and on for thousands of years. Neither side would give in. They fought in every corner of the earth and to the very ends of the universe.

Finally, when it seemed that the whole universe would be destroyed, the demons managed to defeat the Gods. They captured them and imprisoned them under the waters of a deep lake.

Then the Creator called Vritra to him. 'What do you mean to do to my sons the Gods?' he asked.

'Remove them from the universe,' replied Vritra. 'It is the only way to make peace.'

'I cannot allow that,' said the Creator. 'They are my sons too. You must release them.'

'Very well, my father,' Vritra replied. 'But you must give us the power to rule the universe.'

The Creator shook his head. 'To rule over the universe you must have the agreement of all my creations,' he said. 'You must ask them if they want to be ruled by you.'

No-one agreed. No-one wanted to be ruled by the dark powers of the demons.

Still Vritra delayed. 'I will free the Gods,' he said. 'One by one, but only if someone agrees to remain underwater in the lake until they have all been freed. If that person comes up for air then those Gods who remain under water will be my captives forever.'

Vritra was pleased with his plan. He thought no one would be able to stay under water long enough to allow more than a few Gods to escape.

But one man came forward. The Rishi Dadhyang disappeared under the water of the lake and Vritra began, very slowly to free the Gods, one by one. First he released Indra. There was no sign of the Rishi. Then he set free Surya, the Sun God. There was still no sign of the Rishi so, still very slowly, Vritra freed Vayu the Wind God, Agni the God of Fire, Brihaspati...

The Rishi remained underwater until all the Gods were free.

Vritra could not understand how this was possible and sent some of the demons under the water to look for the Rishi. At the very bottom of the lake they found his dead body. The wise man had sacrificed his own life for the sake of the Gods. Vritra was of course furious.

The Gods were happy to be free but very sad to see that the Rishi was dead. They took his body to their father.

'What shall we do with him?' they asked.

'Because of his great sacrifice the Rishi Dadhyang's body has great powers,' replied the Creator. 'If you make a weapon from his bones it will be the strongest ever made. The demons will never again be able to defeat you and the Gods and they will never rule over the heavens.'

And that is what happened. The mighty weapon was called the *vajra* and with its help the Gods killed Vritra and drove the demons from heaven to live in the underworld.

☆☆☆☆☆

Anirudha and Usha

The Mahabharata War was over. Slowly the earth had healed from this war of all wars. The air that had been heavy with the blood and sweat of soldiers was now sweet and fresh. Instead of death and destruction there was peace and the sights and sounds of life.

Home in his kingdom of Dwarka Lord Krishna's own family had grown and his several wives and children lived happily together. But one day his second son Anirudha decided he should see more of the world and he set off in his chariot.

He travelled far to many lands, meeting many different people and seeing strange and wonderful sights. But nothing prepared him for what he saw next.

He had travelled beyond the borders of the earth to the underworld. A thick darkness fell around him and the air turned cold and damp. He could see nothing and he lost all sense of where he was going as he searched for a way back.

After a time which seemed like hours but could have been only minutes, he saw a faint light. He dismounted from his chariot not knowing if he was walking into greater danger or safety but, as he came nearer the light, the darkness began to lift and it became easier to breathe.

Then, not far ahead, he saw the most beautiful woman he had ever seen. She looked like a princess, dressed in rich robes encrusted with precious jewels. On her head she wore a tiara that gleamed with diamonds and rubies and her wrists and ankles were circled in gold.

But it was not her clothes that so attracted Anirudha. It was her beauty and he fell instantly in love with her. As he lost his heart he also lost his head. Without thought of right and wrong, he took hold of her by the wrist and led her back to his chariot to take her home to Dwarka.

The princess at first went quietly with him as in a dream. All she saw was a handsome stranger who somehow dared to kidnap her and take her away from her home. And as she thought this she was suddenly very afraid.

'Help me, Father,' she screamed and pulled away from Anirudha to huddle in a corner of the chariot as it raced along.

Very soon, Anirudha saw that a party of soldiers were following him and he turned quickly and shot a thousand arrows in their direction. Many of the soldiers were killed and Anirudha raced on with Usha still cowering behind him.

But then a great bellow of rage echoed around them as the great figure of Narkasur, Lord of the Underworld emerged from his castle. His heavy-lidded eyes were red with fury, his nostrils were flared and his teeth were bared in a snarl. At each step the ground beneath his feet trembled with a noise like thunder.

'Who is this that dares to take my daughter Usha and kill my warriors?' he roared and summoned his entire army to do battle.

Terrible creatures emerged from the shadows at his command, a hundred thousand of them, intent only on doing his will. Anirudha fought back bravely but he knew he had no chance against such an enemy and it was not long before he was taken prisoner, dragged back to the palace and condemned to death.

Meanwhile, in another part of her father's palace, the princess heard of his fate. She had recovered a little from her shock and remembering how gentle he had been, how handsome and how brave, she decided to help him. She went to her father.

'Father, must this human die only for having fallen in love with me?' she asked. 'Surely, it is not so great a sin?'

Narkasur was astounded that his daughter should challenge him. 'Usha, you waste my time,' he barked. 'My decision is made.'

But Usha was determined. 'Oh Father but think again. Have not many men before him fallen prey to the charms of women without willing or wishing it? Can you not show a little mercy?' She lowered her eyes, suddenly fearful that she had gone too far.

To her surprise her father laughed. 'Very well, my daughter. He will not die today. Instead he will languish in my dungeons and die a lingering death. Guards, take him away.'

Anirudha was thrown into the dark dungeons where he remained in chains for many months. He saw no one but the demons who threw down his food and laughed at him. He thought of his beautiful home in Dwarka. He missed his parents and his brothers. But most of the time he thought of Usha.

Usha could not forget Anirudha either. Glad that she had saved him from death, she knew that life in the dungeons was harsh and that he must be suffering. At last she decided to find out for herself how he was.

She sent away her ladies-in-waiting, dressed herself in a servant's clothes and sneaked past the guards into Anirudha's cell.

Anirudha felt that Usha was near before he saw her. He turned his head but still he thought he was in a dream. Then, she approached him and her sweet smell told him she was really there.

Usha saw with pain how pale and thin Anirudha had become but she looked at his still handsome face and the hand that had so gently yet firmly circled her wrist. She felt a warmth towards him that no princess should feel for her father's prisoner. She was afraid it might be love.

She waited a week before she visited again At first she stood in a dark corner but Anirudha called to her.

'Will you not come closer, princess? I know you are there. Your radiance gives you away.'

Still she did not move.

'Do not be afraid,' he urged her. 'I will not hurt you.'

Usha stepped closer to him. 'Are you well?' she asked.

'Now that I have seen you I am,' replied Anirudha softly.

'I have brought you some food,' she said and gave him a small packet of sweetmeats she had saved from her own dinner.

After this, she visited often and each time took some food so that Anirudha slowly regained his strength. They talked of many things and though they never said so, each knew that they were falling in love.

But Usha knew this was not enough. While she was free and lived a life of comfort and luxury Anirudha still lay on stones in darkness and in dirt.

'Will your family not be very worried about you, my dear Anirudha?' she asked one day.

Anirudha smiled. 'It is not unexpected for one of Krishna's family to stay away on his travels for a long time,' he replied.

Usha could not believe her ears. 'You are of Lord Krishna's family?'

'He is my father,' nodded Anirudha. 'I am his second son.'

'But that is wonderful! All we have to do is get word to him and he will come and rescue you.'

But Anirudha shook his head. 'I have thought long about this,' he said. 'But my fate is here with you.'

'Then both of us will escape together,' replied Usha. 'I know a secret way out of this prison, I shall have a chariot waiting and we will go to your family and be married.'

Still Anirudha did not agree. 'Only a coward runs away,' he said. 'And if we did escape, your father would follow us to Dwarka. I cannot bring such danger to my land. Only, if your father gives you to me in marriage, can we leave.'

'That he will never do,' said Usha sadly. 'He would execute you at once if I asked him.' She continued to try to persuade Anirudha of her plan to send a message to Dwarka, but he resisted and at last she left the dungeon in despair.

She did not visit Anirudha again for several days. She did not go out at all but sat in her chamber, gazing hopelessly from her window until one day, as she was watching the changing of the palace guards, she had an idea.

Her first thought was to share her idea with Anirudha but then she realised he might disagree and she must carry out her plan alone. She summoned the head guard to her room. He entered and bowed his head low in respect.

'How proud you stand there,' Usha declared and the guard raised his chin very slightly, pleased at this compliment. But Usha continued. 'So proud and yet you have not thought to defend me.'

The guard looked up briefly, confused by the change in his princess's voice.

Usha's golden bangles jangled as she held up her hands. 'These hands that wear pure gold are pure no more,' she declared. 'They are dirtied by the touch of a human being. But neither you nor any of your comrade guards has risen to avenge my honour.' She paused to see the effect of her words.

The guard was shuffling from one foot to another, his head hanging in shame. Usha put the last part of her plan into play.

'You pride yourself on your fearlessness and your honour as a soldier,' she said. 'Yet you are afraid to take up my cause. Against a mere mortal. And do you know who he is? A Prince of Dwarka, a land so weak and timid that they do not come to rescue even their own prince. Is there no one here who will defend me against such a country of weaklings? No party of brave *asuras* who will storm their gates and tell them what their son has done for which he now rots in our dungeons? But I waste my words for I know that there is none. You may go.'

Usha had used her words well. Before the day was ended the guard was on his way to Dwarka where the news of Anirudha's imprisonment spread like wildfire amongst the people. They were enraged that the demons would dare to treat their prince in such a way.

Anirudha's father, Lord Krishna, was on his way back to his kingdom after spending some years in deep meditation in an ashram. When he arrived, he found his people in a fury and his brother Balram calling together a large army. Together the brothers led the army out to do battle.

It was at the break of dawn when they reached the gates of the underworld a few days later. They all stood in silence, a magnificent sight in their battle dress, keen to fight, determined to rescue Anirudha. Then the sound of the Dwarka battle horn broke the morning calm.

The sea of soldiers began to surge forward, their steps led by the beating of tambours and drums, the ground beneath them trembling as if in fear. At the gate of Narkasur's palace they stopped. The demon king came out onto his balcony and saw Krishna and Balram at the head of their huge army. He quickly hid his surprise.

'Well well,' he said. 'If it isn't the city of Dwarka at my gates. I would have sent a welcoming party. To what do I owe this pleasure?'

Krishna replied calmly. 'Come down and let us talk like civilised human beings.'

Narkasur was enraged. 'No one tells Narkasur what to do,' he bellowed. 'And you are in my kingdom and at my mercy.'

'Release my son,' Krishna demanded. 'Your punishment is too severe. It is unjust.'

'It is my kingdom,' repeated Narkasur. 'Where I decide what is just.'

'Return to me my son or I will destroy you,' insisted Krishna.

'It is you who will be destroyed,' snarled Narkasur.

The two armies went to war. Each side won small battles but neither gained the upper hand for long. On and on they fought, a whole month passing by. Krishna himself tried only to destroy Narkasur, but the demon king was an expert in warfare and never seemed to tire.

At last he managed to injure Krishna and to damage his bow. He was ready to kill him and claim victory. He lifted his hand to hurl his spear towards him. It was to be the last thing he did.

With all his strength, Krishna stood and called on his divine power, the Sudharshan Chakra. The brilliant disc appeared in the sky, spinning faster than any eye could see, blinding everyone on the battleground. Both armies stopped fighting.

Narkasur also was dazzled. He dropped his weapons and stood helpless as the disc hurtled towards him. Then there was a sickening thud as his head fell to the ground. Seconds later, his body followed.

The demon army began to flee in all directions as the men of Dwarka cut them down and the battleground became a graveyard. Then Balram and Krishna hurried with their troops to find Anirudha, fearing that he too might have been killed. But when they reached the palace they found the guards confused and afraid.

Usha came forward to meet them and bent low to touch their feet. 'Oh Father,' she said. 'Please pardon these asuras who were only doing their duty. My father imprisoned your son because of me. I am the cause of all this death and destruction.'

'Your people shall be safe,' Krishna promised. 'But take me quickly to my son for I fear for his condition after a whole year in prison.'

Of course Usha had looked after Anirudha well and Krishna found him quite strong and in good spirits. He was overjoyed to see his father and uncle, but very soon he began to feel ashamed for having been the cause of war. He was also unable to face Usha who had lost her father in order to gain his freedom.

But Usha's mother was on his side. 'My daughter loves you,' she said. 'And like any good mother I want her to be happy. So take her as your wife with my blessing.'

And so Usha returned with Anirudha to Dwarka where they were married amid great celebration as peace returned and all was well with the world.

☆☆☆☆☆

The Birth of Kali

Everywhere there was peace. The Gods, the Rishis and human beings all lived in harmony with each other and no evil thoughts came between them. All beings worshipped Dharma, son of Surya the Sun God, and he was all-powerful.

Only his step brother Shani was angry and discontented. He was angry that his father had forbidden him to enter into heaven and jealous of his brother's power. He knew that he was not welcome anywhere in the world.

When the Rishi Kanva's son Pragatha was to be married, Shani decided not to go. Instead he went to visit his guru, the great Shukracharya, to ask for his advice. But he did not tell him the true reason for his visit.

'Oh Guru, it pains me that Brihaspati, Guru of the Gods, is loved all over the world while you receive no respect and honour. I have travelled all over the whole world and everywhere it is the same. He and his disciple, my brother Dharma, are praised when it should be you that is Leader of the World.'

Shukracharya thought hard. He himself had long wanted more power and was jealous of Brihaspati. Then he said: 'Go to Pragatha's wedding in disguise as a dancer and entertain the guests so much that they do not see how time is passing and forget the auspicious hour for the ceremony. Then, when Pragatha and Gathini are married they will come under my influence and their child will bring evil into the world, destroy the peace and overcome Dharma's power.'

Shani could not wait to put his Guru's plan into action. He went home to his wife Mohini and asked her to help him.

'I am going to the mortal world,' he explained, 'If you will come with me you can charm the ladies, the Goddesses and the bride so that they too come under our spell and forget what time it is.'

Shani and Mohini disguised themselves as *gandharvas*, musicians to the Gods, and went to the wedding. Guests were arriving from all directions, on horses, bullocks and on foot. Others came in splendid carriages. The bridegroom, Pragatha, was seated on an elephant, dressed in princely clothes with sandal wood paste on his body and garlanded in flowers. Divine music played and there were so many lights in every place that night had become like day and the lights themselves seemed to dance with joy.

In the marriage hall Dharma waited with the guests to welcome Pragatha to a great golden throne that was covered in sweetly smelling flowers. It was as if they were in heaven. All the Gods were there and the planets, including Chandra the Moon God, joined in singing hymns in praise of Dharma. Vayu the Wind God made the winds blow gently to keep the air fresh and calm.

And when Pragatha arrived he looked like a God himself for he had just spent long days in prayer and Brahma had made his body glow with inner light. No one, not even Dharma, imagined that evil forces were gathering together that would destroy the perfect harmony of the world and drive it into pain and unhappiness.

When Shani and Mohini entered the wedding hall they were soon the centre of attention as everyone looked forward to the entertainment. First Shani told them the story that the dance would tell.

'I shall play Vishnu,' he announced, 'who was so long lost in deep prayer and meditation that Brahma became very angry with him. "You have not followed the divine plan and refused to create," Brahma raged but still Vishnu remained calm and did not move. So Brahma tried another way and created Lakshmi, Goddess of Wealth, to persuade Vishnu to stop his meditation and take her as his wife. My partner will take the part of Lakshmi.'

The wedding guests were entranced by the play. They felt that Vishnu and Lakshmi had themselves appeared before them. They bowed low in worship and forgot why they had gathered together. They did not notice how time was passing.

Suddenly, the whole scene disappeared and from outside they heard Lakshmi's voice crying for help. Everyone rushed to look for her, knocking over the lights and tables of food and trampling the sweet flowers underfoot. Many women fainted and fell to the ground. Even Gathini's eyes were heavy and she was close to sleep. Only Pragatha was unaffected, the power of his long prayers and meditation giving him great strength.

Then Dharma knew that it must be Shani who had somehow come to the wedding, caused so much trouble and delayed the marriage ceremony. But he still did not guess at Shani's true purpose and his own Guru, Brihaspati, had gone to sleep so that his power was much reduced.

Slowly the power of Shani's Guru, Shukracharya, began to take effect. The air became heavy and where before it had seemed like heaven, now it was like a nightmare and all joy and happiness had disappeared. Dharma hastened to restore calm. He began to sing hymns from the Vedas, others joined him and so at last Pragatha and Gathini were married.

They had been married after the auspicious hour but Shukracharya's plan was not complete. He had to ensure that they would create a child while his power lasted and he was worried that Pragatha was strong enough to resist him. He called Shani to him.

'Come with me,' he said. 'We must journey to the underworld and ask for the help of Mahamaya, Goddess of Delusion and Attachment. Only she is strong enough to make him do as we wish.'

In the darkest part of the universe, where there was no light and it was impossible to see anything at all, Shani and Shukracharya came upon the most beautiful temple, the home of Mahamaya. Shukracharya began to sing her praises.

'Oh Mahamaya, you who are always awake, you whose power of maya has such great influence over the universe, we beg you help us restore order. The Gods have taken over creation, everywhere there is peace and harmony. And so the asuras are suffering and unhappy and my pupil Shani has no place to call his own. He too is a God, the son of Surya, yet he is banished from heaven and is not welcome anywhere. It is not fair, it is not just. I wish to restore justice and give Shani his share of power. I wish to bring into the world a being with the power to do this.'

Mahamaya was pleased by Shukracharya's words. 'It shall be so,' she said. 'The son born to Pragatha shall be given the name of Kali and he will become the Lord of his age. Under him Shani will be all-powerful and the asuras will again rule the world. The people will no longer believe in the Gods, they will be weak and stupid.'

When Rishi Kanva understood all that had happened at the wedding of his son he prayed to Agni, God of Fire for help. Agni listened to him and replied but it was in the voice of Mahamaya who said:

'Nothing can undo what has already taken place. Kali will be the Leader of his Age and while he is a child you must care for him for he holds the Wheel of Time. Do not look back, Kanva, but think only of the future. I tell you that the age of Kali too will come to an end and then the auspicious time will come again. The Golden Age when humans will again believe in the Gods will come upon the earth and the cycle of time will be complete.'

☆☆☆☆☆

The Ascent of the Pandavas

After the Great War of Mahabharata the Pandavas worked long and hard to restore the happiness and well-being of their kingdom. They began with an *Ashwamedha Yajna*, the horse sacrifice ceremony, and then rebuilt Hastinapur, replacing ruins with new buildings and replanting gardens and parks. Their great friend and ally, Lord Krishna also held a *yajna* to fill the world with love and friendship.

The newfound sense of peace and joy was not what Kali had planned. Where he wanted sorrow and discord he saw the Pandava kingdom restored to a heaven on earth. Where he needed there to be fear, greed, jealousy and dispute he heard the voices of the people once again full of hope and life and laughter. He went to seek the help of his uncle, the Rishi Durvasa.

The Rishi was famous for his spiritual energy but also for his extremely bad temper. He became angry at the smallest offence and his curses were powerful and always came true, so no one dared to upset him. He promised to help his nephew.

Meanwhile there were great celebrations after the completion of the second *yajna*. Everyone was in high spirits enjoying the return of peace and prosperity. One of Lord Krishna's sons, a little under the influence of alcohol, dressed as a woman, tied an iron ball to his stomach and pretended to be expecting a baby. His drunken friends dragged him to the Rishi and asked him to guess whether the baby would be a boy or a girl.

The Rishi was not fooled and he knew the boys were trying to make fun of him and his powers. He flew into a great rage and called down a curse on their whole clan. It was not long before the Yadavs began to fight and kill each other until the only male member of the clan remaining was Vajra, Krishna's infant great grandson.

When the Pandavas learned that the Yadavs had left this world, they decided they too would give up their beautiful kingdom and leave for heaven. They felt lost without Krishna's wisdom and spiritual guidance and knew that Kali would soon be all-powerful. And so the five brothers and their wife, Draupadi, cast off their royal satins and silks and all their adornments and, dressed in simple ascetic robes, began the long and difficult ascent to heaven.

Yudhisthir, the eldest and wisest led the way, followed by his brothers Bhima, Arjun, Nakul and Sahdeva, with their wife and Queen, Draupadi, behind them. Their first task was to find the secret gateway in the mountains where the peaks were always covered in snow.

'My beloved brothers, my dear wife, the journey will be long and dangerous,' Yudhisthir warned. 'But whatever happens we must continue.'

It was windy and bitterly cold, blinding snow surrounded them and the narrow paths were strewn with rocks and deep crevices. It would have been only too easy to fall, yet Yudhisthir never faltered and he remained full of energy.

Bhima, who had always been the strongest of the brothers, was astonished. 'Brother, please slow down,' he begged. 'We cannot keep up with you. Let us take a little rest.'

But Yudhisthir refused and after a time they did all manage to reach the secret gates that would lead them to heaven. However, here the way became even more difficult. It became still colder and with every step they were more tired and every breath was a strain. Finally Draupadi could go no further. She fell to the ground.

'Do not leave me alone,' she pleaded. 'Give me a hand.'

All the brothers but Yudhisthir turned to help her. 'Do not stop,' he ordered them. 'Or you will not reach your goal.' Then he addressed Draupadi. 'Dear wife, you have more strength than you know,' he said. 'Look ahead to the joys waiting for you in heaven and have faith in yourself.'

To her surprise, Draupadi was able to stand and continue but soon she again fell and this time she was unable to recover and knew she would die.

'Your body is weak,' Yudhisthir consoled her. 'But your spirit is strong and nothing can destroy you. Let go your body and you will reach heaven.'

Draupadi did as Yudhisthir advised her, closed her eyes and relaxed. She forgot the cold and the pain, her body became still and finally her soul left her body.

The brothers were shocked at the death of Draupadi for they had all loved her very much. Bhima in particular could not understand why she had not been able to attain heaven in her own body since she had lived a blameless life and been an ideal wife to them all.

'She had made one small mistake which reduced her strength at the end,' Yudhisthir explained. 'She secretly loved Arjun more than any of us. He was her soul mate. So she was living a lie when she told us she loved us all the same.'

Next Sahdeva began to weaken and soon knew that his journey too had come to an end. Again Yudhisthir advised him to discard his body without regret and set free his soul. This time Bhima was angry.

'Our brother always respected you and guided us all with his special gift of foresight,' he said. 'And now you abandon him. Why did he fail to complete this journey?'

'He too made one mistake,' replied Yudhisthir. 'In the Mahabharata War, when we sent our nephew Abhimanyu on his last fatal mission, Sahdeva knew he would fail and, out of pride in his superior knowledge, he did not warn us.'

Bhima was silent as he remembered the pain of losing Abhimanyu when, without weapons to defend himself, he was caught and killed by seven Kaurava warriors.

It was not long before Nakul too fell to the ground and he too was advised by Yudhisthir to have no fear. Once again Bhima questioned his brother for he knew that Yudhisthir had loved Nakul best.

'What was his sin that he could not reach heaven in his physical body?' he asked.

'Nakul was blessed with good looks in which he took great pride,' replied Yudhisthir. 'His was the sin of vanity.'

The three remaining Pandavas continued on their journey. As if it was not difficult enough, a great danger suddenly appeared in their path as a terrifying giant demon towered over them.

'My name is Kamadwish,' he thundered. 'And I am here to end your journey. For Yama, the God of Death, himself decrees that no mere mortal may continue beyond this point. Obey or I shall enjoy feasting on your measly bodies.'

'But we are not mere mortals,' replied Yudhisthir calmly. 'We are the sons of Gods on earth. I myself am a representative of Lord Yama and have spent my life spreading the divine message among all the people of the world. Move aside or face your own end.'

Kamadwish was at first surprised. Never before had any human being threatened him. But then his eyes began to burn with anger and power surged through his body as it expanded to its full and dreadful size. Yudhisthir ordered Bhima to destroy him.

The battle was tremendous as each pitted their great strength against the other. Mountains trembled, the skies opened up and the clouds burst with lightning and deafening claps of thunder. But Bhima overcame the monster, who knocked down several mountain tops with him as he fell.

As the three brothers continued on their way they noticed that a dog had begun to follow and keep pace with them no matter how fast they walked. Then Arjun weakened. Bravest of all the Pandavas, he too became exhausted. He fell down to the ground without even calling to his brothers.

Bhima was heartbroken. 'Do you not stop to grieve even for Arjun who won every war for us?' he cried. 'What possible sin can he have committed?'

'Dear brother,' said Yudhisthir. 'Arjun was a great warrior and took pride in his godly strength. But he lost faith in himself when the Yadavs were destroyed and Krishna left this world. And so his strength became his weakness. That is why he could not complete this journey. But listen! Do you hear that music?'

Bhima listened and, despite all his sadness and the hardship he had endured, was filled with joy. 'What is this instrument that makes my heart sing with happiness?' he asked.

'It is the instrument of the Gods that came from the churning of the oceans,' Yudhisthir replied. 'This means we are very near our goal. We are approaching the doors of heaven.'

Bhima's great happiness did not last long. He collapsed, suddenly overcome by the cold and exhaustion. But even as he lay dying he wanted to know why, like his brothers, he had failed to reach heaven in his bodily form.

'Dear Bhima, you are very pure,' said Yudhisthir. 'Your only fault was your complete honesty. You did not realise that sometimes telling the truth causes pain. This was your only sin.'

Now, Yudhisthir was alone except for the faithful dog. Suddenly, it was as if he was in a different country. The frozen mountains disappeared, and the cold wind gave place to a gentle breeze. Where there had been dangerous rocks, flowers of every colour bloomed and there were trees of gold with sapphire blue leaves. On either side of the path were beautiful lakes where lotus flowers floated and swans glided. The air was filled with the hum of life.

Yudhisthir felt he was in paradise. But then he saw that his way was blocked by a group of beautiful *apsaras,* divine dancers with complexions of molten gold and long flowing hair. They begged him to stay with them.

'We will serve you,' they promised. 'And like us you will remain young for ever.'

Yudhisthir resisted. He knew this must be a test of his strength and, politely refusing their request, walked on. Twice more he was distracted, first by a group of men who all wanted to speak to and delay him and next by a group of Gandharvas, semi-divine beings, who invited him to rest awhile with them.

Both times he held fast to his decision and walked on until he came to a river which he knew must be the river of heaven, the Mandakini. He bent to drink and immediately felt well and full of energy as he had never felt before. It was as if he was filled with pure joy. Then across the river he saw his final destination: the place where Lord Yama or Dharma lived. But how was he to cross the river? He sat down on the bank to consider.

Meanwhile Lord Indra, King of the Gods was holding court. 'See, Yudhisthir has reached the banks of the Mandakini,' he said. 'Let us go and welcome him. He shall ride with me in my chariot to cross the river and then enter heaven.'

When the Gods saw that Yudhisthir was not alone they were horrified. 'No dog can enter heaven,' they said. 'For they are impure creatures.'

'He is my faithful companion,' replied Yudhisthir. 'I cannot leave him behind.'

'Your virtue has given you the right to enter into heaven. Do not waste it for the sake of a mere dog,' Lord Indra urged him.

Yudhisthir again refused and then Indra relented, agreeing that the dog could share in Yudhisthir's great virtue. The dog jumped into the carriage and, at that very moment, was transformed into none other than Lord Yama.

'I wished to see how you would fare against such obstacles along the way,' he said. 'And I am especially pleased that you refused to abandon your companion.'

But Yudhisthir was sad. 'Why are my brothers and Draupadi not yet in heaven?' he asked.

'They are in hell,' replied Indra. 'But it is only for a short time.'

'Let me join them,' Yudhisthir begged. 'Until such time as we may all ascend together into heaven.'

'This cannot be,' replied Yama. 'For you have committed no sin. But perhaps we may forgive your wife and brothers and let them immediately join you here.'

And so the ascent of the Pandavas, which had begun with such hardship and danger ended as the five brothers and their devoted queen were reunited in heaven where they lived together in great tranquillity and joy for many thousands of years.

☆☆☆☆☆

King Parikshit and the Wandering Rishi

The Pandavas left their kingdom in the hands of Arjun's grandson Parikshit. When he had overcome his grief at the loss of his elders, he became one of the greatest kings in the world.

This was a time when every great king had a council of wise men to advise them. This council included Rishis who, being very devout with strong moral values, did not wish for power and position for themselves. Their actions were not driven by any selfish interests and years of *tapasya,* of study and an austere way of living, had given them immense powers and special insight. Their advice was very valuable to the King.

One of King Parikshit's most wise advisors was Rishi Jaratkaru. He had great mental and spiritual powers and his advice was always sought on the most important matters of the kingdom. The other Rishis admired him as much as did the King but he had not long been part of the council and they wanted to know more about him. One day Jaratkaru told them his story.

'My parents died when I was only eight years old,' he said, 'and I thought I was doomed to a life of misery. But then my Guru took me into his ashram and cared for me as a son. He taught me to seek peace within myself for all of us must one day die and leave this world. He said that I must spend my time in *tapasya* and meditation and after some time, having acquired spiritual powers, I became a wandering Rishi.

'Sometimes I sat in the burning sands of the desert but I felt no heat. Sometimes I found myself in remote snow-covered mountains but I felt no cold. I lost all sense of time and place, and often was not conscious of my physical self and felt no desire or attachment. All I thought of was the divine. I felt complete. In all my wanderings, I felt no hunger or thirst or fear. Many times I met with a ferocious lion or tiger, but when I bowed down to them they left me alone to continue on my way. But then something happened to change my life.'

Jaratkaru paused while his audience shifted and again made themselves comfortable.

'One day I heard a feeble voice repeating my name,' he continued. 'The voice was so faint that I had to listen hard. This is what I heard.

'Oh Jaratkaru, our souls are damned for eternity for you are our only descendant and you have forgotten us.'

'I looked around me and at last saw a tiny figure at my feet and behind it five others hanging as from a spider's thread in the air.

'"I am your father," said the first creature, "and these are your ancestors. You have chosen a solitary path in life and found great joy. But for us, if you do not marry, if you do not have a son it means complete annihilation, the end of our connection to the world."

'I was deeply moved by my father's plea,' Jaratkaru continued. 'I asked him how shall I find a wife for I have no place to live, nor any possessions to share with her. But my father assured me that I would find a girl and that I should accept her. And it was not long before I did receive an offer of marriage. From Vasuki, King of the Nagas, the snakes, who wished me to marry his sister Mansa.'

A great gasp and an angry mutter arose from Jaratkaru's listeners. No one could believe that the Snake King could make such a proposal. But Jaratkaru held up his hand for silence.

'I too could not understand how Vasuki could suggest the wedding of two such different species,' he said, 'but the king explained that his race was doomed to extinction unless his sister married someone with great spiritual power. It was a long story, but after hearing it, I took pity on him for his situation was so similar to my own. So I accepted the marriage offer but I made certain conditions.

'You all know that the Nagas are known for their bad temper? Well, I said that Mansa must learn to control her weaknesses such as anger, desire and greed, for I hate these evils. Secondly, I said she must take my name, and finally that she must not expect me to stay with her once she has conceived a child. I shall then depart to resume my spiritual life.

'Vasuki agreed, the wedding took place and for some time all was well. Although it was hard for Mansa, she did manage to control her temper and our life together was peaceful. But then one day she made me very angry. Every day just before sunset I meditate and pray. Indeed, I believed the sun would not set without me doing so.

'But this day came, when I was sleeping with my head in Mansa's lap and I did not waken. Finally, seeing that the sun had almost set, she woke me and I, seeing how my powers had diminished, that the sun would set without me, blamed her. Our marriage had distracted me from my spiritual path and I left her.

'I would not have gone back had not Vasuki followed me and reminded me that my family too was doomed to extinction if I had no son. So I did return and Mansa did give birth to a son and then I left, returned to my wanderings and came here.'

There was an uneasy silence as Jaratkaru stopped speaking. His story did not quite have the ending his listeners had hoped for. At last, one of his fellow councillors raised his hand. 'Please tell us, great Rishi, what became of the boy, your son?'

Jaratkaru smiled. 'He was named Astik and he was truly the son of a Rishi,' he said proudly. 'For at the age of eight he left his mother and dedicated himself to a life of *tapasya*. So great a power did he achieve that his body generated a brilliant energy and light.'

At this, Jaratkaru pointed to a corner of the chamber where the councillors were gathered and there, aglow with his energy and to the amazement and delight of the whole assembly, stood Astik, the son who would save two races from extinction.

☆☆☆☆☆

Kali and Shani Seek Help

With the departure of both the Yadavs and the Pandavas from this earth Kali was sure that the world was under his control. He thought that now there was no one left who could challenge his powers. But then he heard from his allies, the Nagas that someone was training to use the divine weapons. He went to see for himself.

To his surprise he found that the young king Parikshit was already highly skilled. He could create huge fires with the Agni missile, and terrible storms with the Vayuban, the wind weapon. He could make great showers of stars and bring torrential rain to the battlegrounds so that even his own soldiers had to run to save their lives or be drowned.

Kali was angry but he was also worried. Somehow, the divine forces had preserved their powers through their descendant, Parikshit, who would surely now seek to bring back the laws of righteousness and thwart Kali's plans. He went to see his friend Shani.

'This Parikshit is as skilled in the arts of war as his grandfather Arjun,' he said. 'Unless we do something you will see your great rival Dharma again ruling the world.'

'Let us seek our Guru's help,' said Shani. 'Only he can stop this happening.'

Shukracharya was in deep meditation and quite unaware of recent events. Quickly, Kali told him all that had happened, and cleverly laid the blame on the Guru Brihaspati, knowing that he was Shukracharya's great rival.

'I had followed your advice, Oh Guruji, but the cunning Brihaspati advised the Gods to make a great *yajna*. Through which they gave divine powers to five brothers, the Pandavas, who with the help of Vishnu, in the form of Krishna won a great battle. Their aim was to restore the rule of dharma. Again I succeeded in disrupting their peace and both clans departed this earth leaving a mere boy to rule in their place. King Parikshit.' He spat out the name.

'And you fear this boy?' Shukracharya's anger at the news of Brihaspati's interference seemed about to turn on Kali. Kali hurried to explain.

'He has already learnt to use the divine weapons, Guruji. He will be as powerful as Arjun who with Krishna could have destroyed all creation. He will prevent me taking my rightful place at the Wheel of Time. Unless you help us. For only you, great Guru, can change the course of these events and set the world back on its path of doom and darkness.'

Shukracharya took a deep breath and sunk into contemplation as he considered what to do. By sunset he had a plan. He summoned Kali and Shani. 'Listen to me carefully,' he commanded. 'Follow my instructions and we can undo all that the Gods have gained.'

Kali and Shani leaned forward eagerly.

'You must take every opportunity to make trouble for this boy, Parikshit. He cannot be harmed for he is under the protection of the Rishis Vyasa and Shukdeva. Shukdeva is immune to worldly desires and attachments. I have no influence over him.'

Kali was confused. 'Then what can we do if the boy cannot be touched?'

'Patience!' shouted Shukracharya. Sometimes his disciples annoyed him. 'You must make sure that the people of the world are given every opportunity to defy the rules of creation, to sin against the laws of Brahma. And I will tell you how.' Shukracharya allowed himself a small smile.

'Today's leaders are slaves to their egos,' he continued. 'They demand respect instead of earning it. Use this and other weaknesses against them. Drive them towards drink and wasteful enjoyment and as they drift away from the path of Dharma, of righteousness, reward them with riches beyond their greatest dreams. Encourage those with ill intent. Make Kings of robbers, make Leaders of thieves.' He turned his gaze on Shani and beckoned to him to come closer.

'And you Shani have a special role in this,' he said. 'It is to you that people will pray to grant their wishes. It is your blessings therefore that will lead humanity astray. You must reward the greedy and the godless, bless the wicked, shower the evil with riches. And once they have had a taste of luxury and fortune they will want more, and you will have them under your control.'

Shani nodded eagerly, thrilled at the thought of his great responsibility, but Shukracharya had not finished.

'And besides all this, you must use your great powers to bring disease and despair. Of course there will be some who continue to follow the path of Dharma but these you must drive to complete ruination. The more they practise religion, the more you must torment them. The more faithful they are, the more they must suffer until eventually they will become so wretched that they too can be corrupted.'

Shukracharya gave an evil laugh. 'And even the religious leaders will be not be spared. They will become greedy for money and power, and people will lose faith in them and their belief in religion, until every last bit of godliness has disappeared from the human race. '

Kali bent low at his guru's feet. 'You are so wise, Guruji. Only you could have thought of such a plan that cannot fail. Only -' he hesitated. 'I have one question. How do I defeat Parikshit? How can I pull him from his circle of protection?'

Shukracharya smiled. 'You really must learn patience, Kali,' he said. 'The time will come. And when it does, even Shukdeva will not be able to save him.'

☆☆☆☆☆

The Snake Sacrifice

At the beginning of Kaliyuga, there were giant serpents much bigger and more terrifying than those we know today. As his allies, Kali had given them the task of poisoning the earth's atmosphere and of spreading sickness and despair. He told them to destroy goodness wherever they found it and so the Rishis in particular were constantly under their attack.

The snakes hid in the houses of these holy men and drank their precious ghee without which the Rishis could not light the holy fire. They attacked their cows, drank their sacred milk and bit and poisoned them. Anyone who played the smallest part in a *yajna* also became their victim.

One day King Parikshit, together with thousands of Brahmins, was listening to the Rishi Shukdeva tell the story of the Bhagwata Purana. None of them knew that one of the Brahmins was Takshak, son of the Snake King Arbuda, in disguise. He was there at Kali's request. His purpose was to kill Parikshit.

The story ended as Shukdeva told how Lord Krishna left his mortal body and the entire city of Dwarka was swallowed up by the sea. The assembled Brahmins closed their eyes in sorrow and grief and did not see

Takshak return to his real form. He became a gigantic snake with a thousand hoods. He reared up high over Parikshit and bit him on the top of his head. So deadly was the poison that the King's soul had left his body before he fell lifeless to the ground.

The only person who saw this terrible murder was Parikshit's son, Janmejaya, a boy of eight who then became king. He was so angry that he went around killing snakes wherever he found them until his mother stopped him. But by then, Takshak had already turned himself back into a Brahmin. He walked quietly away into the forest.

Janmejaya never forgot how his father had died, and nor did he forgive the snakes whose attacks on the Rishis became worse and worse. At last, and on Shukdeva's advice, Janmejaya organised a month-long snake sacrifice. Word of this *yajna* spread far and wide. Everyone wished to be rid of the snakes, and rulers of many other kingdoms arrived to take part. Beautiful houses and dining halls were built to accommodate the visitors.

Usually any news of a *yajna* or other religious ceremony would have brought out a plague of snakes to prevent it. But this time, for the very first time, it was the snakes who were afraid. Believing they would all be killed, they hid wherever they could. Some snakes went deep into the oceans, others into the densest forests. They took shelter in cracks in the rocky mountains or tunnelled deep underground. Snakes from all over the world tried to find strength in numbers and coiled together around trees to form solid pillars.

On the day of the *yajna*, the sacrificial fire rose high into the heavens and the Rishis chanted powerful incantations calling upon all the Gods to be present to help pull the snakes from their hiding places towards the flames. There, Janmejaya was waiting with the divine weapons to cut them into pieces.

More and more snakes were consumed by the roaring fire and it seemed that the end of their whole race could not be far away. The power of the *yajna* was so strong that it even shook the mighty Vasuki, the overall Lord of the Nagas who held up the earth on his great hood and therefore enjoyed the special protection of the Gods.

Vasuki felt himself to be safe, but he feared the destruction of the rest of his race. As the chants of the *yajna* grew louder and louder, and more and more snakes were killed, he remembered his nephew Astik, son of his sister Mansa and the Rishi Jaratkaru and himself now a powerful Rishi. He called on King Arbuda to seek Astik's help.

Meanwhile, even the mighty Takshak felt himself being dragged towards the fire. He coiled himself around the throne of Kali, hoping that its colossal weight would save him. It was of course at Kali's command that he had killed Parikshit and caused the deadly *yajna* to take place.

But the chanting of the Rishis was so full of power that Takshak and Kali and his great throne were all pulled closer and closer to the flames until Takshak could feel their heat on his scales. He closed his eyes as he awaited his certain destruction.

'Stop!' A clear voice rang out.

Takshak realised that he had stopped moving. He opened his eyes to see that Kali's throne, with himself coiled round it, was suspended in mid-air over the sacrificial fire.

The Rishis had ceased their chanting, their hands suddenly still where they had been ladling ghee into the fire, and the crowd turned in stunned silence to see who had spoken. Who could have the power to utter such a command? Surely no *yajna* once begun had ever been stopped?

There at the entrance stood a Rishi, hair matted like the other Rishis, but larger than life, tall and strong, his body radiating pure white light, his voice deep and hypnotic.

'This *yajna* shall continue no further,' he announced. 'And you, Takshak, shall be safe for a long, long, time under the protection of Kali.'

The chief Rishi protested. 'Why, oh Rishi, have you halted our sacred rites? Why do you protect this Naga when it is he who killed our beloved King Parikshit? Explain yourself.'

The Rishi stepped closer. 'My name is Astik,' he told them. 'Remember, I am the nephew of Arbuda and also of Vasuki who holds on his head our mother earth. And I have come to save the race of snakes from utter destruction. And I have also come to save you from yourself, O Rishi.'

The Rishi still did not understand.

'Do you not know that destruction of any creature or race goes against the will of Brahma and will make him angry? Do you want every Brahmin to become the enemy of Brahma? Did you not think, O Sages, that a *yajna* as powerful as this would make even Vasuki tremble, so that the world would lose its balance and the whole universe might be destroyed? Please reconsider and do not continue with your chanting.'

The Rishis turned to each other to discuss what they should do but Janmejaya approached Astik.

'Do you not know what a menace the snakes have become to everyone?' he asked. 'How they attack even the Rishis and their cows? Besides recently killing Lord Krishna's grandson, Vajra, in Mathura and my own father Parikshit? And listen, Astik, your own father Jaraktaru, who as you know is a member of my Assembly of Councillors, was one of those who agreed to hold this *yajna*. So we will halt the ceremony while we consult the Assembly, and only if they agree with you, will I stop it altogether.'

Janmejaya took Astik to meet the Assembly where he again explained why no one had the right to destroy a whole race.

'We understand your reason,' a senior Rishi spoke up. 'But if we stop the *yajna* the snakes will again terrorise the people, pollute the atmosphere and prevent our religious ceremonies. No one can stop them.'

Then Astik replied. 'I promise you all that they will do so no longer. They will not attack anyone nor offend the Rishis. I give you my word that they will live apart from and in peace with the rest of creation.'

And so it was. Janmejaya ended the *yajna,* the crowds who had travelled from far and wide went home, and the wonderful buildings that had been constructed for them became a new city, named in honour of its first king. It is called Jaipur.

When King Janmejaya Met Kali

King Janmejaya was a good and brave king. One day he heard from his Guru, Shukdeva and the powerful Rishi Vyasa that Kaliyuga, the Iron Age or Age of Kali, was almost upon the world.

'In this Age, O Janmejaya, most people will not believe in Gods,' Vyasa told him. 'They will worship only money and pleasure. Wealth will belong only to those people who worship these two powers.'

Of course Janmejaya was very worried and Vyasa continued. 'The world will be divided into smaller and smaller nations and there will be more and more conflicts between them. Even between communities, between parents and their children there will be so much discord that life will not seem worth living. Life will be without peace, without hope.'

On hearing these terrible words, Janmejaya was determined to fight against Kali's power. He travelled all over India teaching the message of the Mahabharata to all the people so that they would be better prepared for the dark days to come. He told how, in their war with the Kauravas, the Pandavas always told the truth, however difficult the situation became, and took the right decisions without hesitation. They never chose the easy way out.

Janmejaya made this his life's work. Once he had answered the people's questions he moved on to another part of India, and in this way spent several years. But what he really wanted was to destroy Kali completely.

One day something very strange happened. He was walking through a thick forest near the river Ganges when he saw a cowherd beating his cow. The poor cow was standing on only one leg because its other three legs were broken. King Janmejaya was very angry and ordered the boy to stop his cruelty but the cowherd continued beating the cow. The King drew his sword to attack the cowherd, but at this moment the whole sight disappeared.

Suddenly, the King heard loud laughter and a voice came from above. 'O Janmejaya, I am Kali, Lord of the Iron Age, and what you thought was a cow is Dharma, God of Righteousness, of religion. Know that in this age, it is only I, who will be the most powerful. If you wish to have any success in life, any prosperity, you must bow down before me and worship me. If you do so, your happiness and joy will be boundless and your problems will vanish as if they had never been. If you do not, you will never have a day of peace but suffer endless sorrows and disappointments. This is my Age, I am the Time.'

Then Kali showed himself before Janmejaya. He was enormous, terrifying, dark as the night. It was if a massive thundercloud had appeared in front of the king. His three eyes were red and burned like coals. In his four hands he carried a bow and arrow, a spear and a drinking vessel. On his head, he wore a dazzling crown of jewels, and a python was wound round his neck like a garland. His voice was loud as thunder.

'Remember this, Janmejaya, worship me and you will have peace, happiness and success in all your ventures. But if you do not, only pain and defeat await you at every step of the way.'

Janmejaya was not afraid, even at so strange and frightening a sight. He was glad to have seen Kali face to face and even more determined to destroy him and throw him out of creation.

'I do not believe you, Kali,' he said. 'I think you are only a magician who frightens people into believing in your power. Give me a little time and I will return and destroy you.'

Janmejaya hurried away to seek the help of his friend King Shiladitya. This King was very surprised to hear that Kali was in the forest near his own kingdom and very glad to join forces with Janmejaya. Together with their armies they marched to the attack.

When Kali saw them coming, there streamed out from his body an immensely powerful evil force yet the two kings did not hesitate and together they overpowered Kali. However, he managed to escape and from a distance came his threatening voice.

'Our battle is not over. When the time comes, I shall return and take my revenge. And the time will be when I choose.'

Yet Janmejaya and Shiladitya believed they had defeated Kali once and for all. They were overjoyed and to celebrate their victory they planned to build a great city on the site of the battle. They called it Kalicut, Kolkata as it is now known.

Janmejaya returned home and told his guru, Shukdeva, all about his adventures. But Shukdeva did not rejoice. He told his pupil, the King, that what Kali had said was true and that there was no way he could be defeated.

'The real war is to come,' he told Janmejaya. 'Time is divided between the rule of Satyadeva, Lord of Truth and that of Kali and it is Kali's time. He will return.'

Janmejaya was horrified. 'Then tell me, Guruji. I have told you how I saw Kali in the person of the cowherd beating the cow. Tell me the meaning of the fourth leg on which the cow was still standing.'

'It is a symbol of the effort that humans make to discover the Divine,' replied Shukdeva. 'Their prayers, their sacrifices. Such efforts are always under attack by Kali.'

'But how can the cow stand on one leg?' asked Janmejaya. 'Is there no hope that we may one day defeat Kali and the power of the Divine will return?'

'Listen, O King, with a quiet mind,' replied Shukdeva. 'Kali will gain full victory over the earth. He has the help of Shukracharya, the Guru of the Asuras, and of Shani the enemy of truth and of religion. People will not be able to recognise the truth even when it is in front of them. Their minds will be full of delusions. They will be terrified and feel helpless in the face of death, for Dharma, religion and all spiritual activities, will have lost their power.'

Many years passed. One day Shukdeva told Janmejaya that he had seen Kali wandering in the city and that this was the best time to attack him. Together they went to find Kali, Janmejaya carrying the divine bow, the *Gandiva*, and Shukdeva the *Brahmadand*, the fearsome weapon of Lord Brahma himself. It was so dark that they could not see each other. Suddenly they heard Kali's voice.

'Now is your chance to fight me, Janmejaya,' he thundered. 'Let us see who is the most powerful.'

Janmejaya felt a deep dread. In the darkness he could see only the unearthly light of Kali's jewels. Still, he did not lose courage and with the Gandiva let fly thousands of arrows which lit up the forest as they flew towards Kali. But Kali was ready with his Trident which destroyed as many arrows as Janmejaya fired.

'You see, King of the World,' he laughed. 'I am winning. I will destroy you, however hard you fight. Bow down before me or I will kill you.'

Then Shukdeva was very angry. 'Death is better than worshipping you, Kali,' he said. 'And if our death occurs on the battlefield we will go straight to heaven.'

So saying, brave Shukdeva hurled the Brahmadand at Kali. As it left his hand a great light shone and it went straight to its target. But the Trident cast it aside and again Kali laughed.

'You see, great Guru, my power is greater than that of Brahma himself. It is Brahma that has decided that this Age will be mine and in my Age no power will be greater than my Trident.'

'O four-armed Kali,' replied Janmejaya. 'We see how powerful you are. But look, I cast aside my weapon. Do the same and let us fight with our bare hands. Only then will it be a fair fight. I know that if you defeat me your Age will begin but I believe I can defeat you for I am the Truth, I follow Dharma and I do only good deeds.'

Janmejaya's brave words enraged Kali. He threw aside his Trident and began to hit him with his fists. He hit him so hard and for so long that the King's whole body lost its shape and he was no more. Thus Janmejaya lost his final battle with Kali and Shukdeva, to avoid Kali's power, went to live in the Himalayas far from the rest of the world.

☆☆☆☆☆

Vivekananda in America

The Golden Age has still to arrive but the power of Dharma, of the Truth, has never disappeared completely. It has been preserved and passed on by generations of Gurus and their disciples. Vivekananda was a follower of the Guru Ramakrishna Paramhansa. He travelled from Bengal all over India together with three other disciples to spread the Guru's teachings. He was such a good speaker that many people praised him, but he worried that they did not truly take his message to their hearts and soon forgot what he had said.

One day, in 1893, he heard of the World Conference of Faiths that was going to be held that September in Chicago, USA and he decided to go. America was a new country, he thought, more open to other religions. There were many religions in India but each seemed to think that theirs was the only true one. Vivekananda had learnt from his Guru that there is really no important difference between them.

In Chicago he was given a seat in the Conference but was told that there would be no time for him to speak. At the end of the last day, however, a speaker did not turn up and Vivekananda was asked if he could address the conference instead. It was very short notice but it was the opportunity he had so much wanted. He closed his eyes for a moment and thought of his Guru and silently asked for his help. Keeping in mind the smiling face of Sri Ramakrishna, he began.

'Dear brothers and sisters,' he said, 'I do not have knowledge of any other truth but what I learned from my Guru. I will try to explain what he discovered.' He paused. 'Truth is very strange. One does not listen to truth with one's ears. One does not see it with one's eyes. One does not attain it by reading books. One must discover it in oneself.'

His audience was interested and asked him to tell them what he had discovered.

'My Guru said that in the beginning there was only one religion, one Truth,' he explained. 'But over time and in different places different religions have grown up, each believing it was the only way to reach heaven. But just as each river takes a different path but still they all reach the ocean in the end. In the same way, all religions aim to reach the same goal.'

Vivekananda continued to speak as if he was directly inspired. His torrent of words kept the audience spell-bound. No one noticed how the time was passing until suddenly a bell rang for the end of the conference. Everyone stood and silently left and Vivekananda could not finish his speech. He felt he had failed his Guru and went to his room to try to sleep.

He spent the whole night tossing and turning and decided that he would return to India as soon as possible. Just before dawn he fell asleep and then he saw Sri Ramakrishna smiling at him.

'Your words will be remembered and praised by all people for a long time,' his Guru assured him. 'You have done a great thing.'

When Vivekananda opened his door in the morning he found a great crowd waiting to speak with him. Many carried newspapers which had reports of his speech and photographs of himself on their front page. Finally, the chief organiser of the conference spoke to him.

'Your speech is being reported all over the country,' he told him. 'You won everyone's heart. You must stay longer and give more talks to the people.'

And this is what he did. He taught people how to practise Pranayama, to control their breathing so that they might attain power over their senses and achieve peace and knowledge of the divine soul within themselves.

'With all your senses you will experience divine joy,' he promised. 'Living in this world where there is so much conflict, many of us lead confused and desperate lives. We forget that part in us, the soul, that is divine and become unhappy. Discover it and your life will be full of divine light, peace and happiness. In fact, you will live like a God. '

Vivekananda preached his Guru's message to great numbers of people in the USA and other countries as well. Many people became his followers and disciples and they began to spread his words all over the world.

✯✯✯✯✯

Lord Krishna's Visit to Sri Aurobindo

In 1908, Sri Aurobindo was thrown into Alipore Jail by the British police together with others of his comrades. He was wrongly accused of helping in the killing of two British women.

Locked away, he was unhappy that he could play no part in the movement against British rule of India, and worried about his friends in other cells. He spent most of his time in prison meditating. One night, he noticed a strange light in his cell which became brighter until, in the middle of the light, Aurobindo saw he had a visitor, a young boy, no more than five years old. Dark and beautiful, the child wore silver anklets which tinkled as he moved and a peacock feather on his head. In his hands he carried a flute which filled the dark cell with magical music as from another world.

Sri Aurobindo was confused. 'How have you, a mere child, entered this dark prison?' he said. 'This is no place to play.'

The boy laughed. 'You do not know me! I am Krishna, Lord of the Universe. You have been calling me all the time. I have come to help you.'

'You cannot be that Krishna who fought with the Pandavas at the great battle of Mahabharata,' Aurobindo insisted. 'He is the one power that makes the world, the stars and the planets move. Only he can comfort me.'

Again the boy laughed. 'It is you who speak like a child. Have you not learnt that I come again and again in different *avatars,* different forms, in all the Ages to save the earth? Have you so lost your mind in this jail that you do not know that I take this form when I meet my devotees? Do you not believe me? Watch and you shall see me in my real form.'

As Aurobindo watched the boy was transformed into an immense being with countless arms and legs, and eyes and ears. His hundreds of thousands of feet rested on the earth yet his head was higher than the highest heaven.

'Look at me,' came a voice from the great apparition, 'and you will see the entire universe. My breath gives life to all beings, my sight gives them sight. I am in all human beings, in the secret corners of their hearts. In each I am like a flame, the size of a thumb. I am each person's soul.'

Then, Krishna's child avatar reappeared. 'So now do you believe me? Ask me the questions that trouble you and I will help you.'

Aurobindo spoke with a trembling voice. 'Why then, Lord, do you destroy life? Why is there death and a world where people fear for their lives?'

'There is no death,' replied Krishna. 'All souls are part of me and are therefore eternal. A soul is not born nor does it die. Only the body dies. The body is made of the five elements, air, fire, earth, water and space that come together and then again break apart. Look at the ocean where a wave forms, rushes to the shore and there loses its form. Life and Death are very similar. So do not worry, leave all your cares with me. This is the same advice that I gave Arjun on the battlefield of Kurukshetra.'

Still Aurobindo had one important question. 'Divine Lord, can you free my comrades and me from this terrible prison where we will surely be put to death?'

'This will not happen,' said Krishna. 'And India will soon be free. But it is not only this that I desire, for soon afterwards the Golden Age will begin and India will be the chosen place where you will help bring back the true religion of Dharma. India is like a sleeping lion. When its people wake up, they will again live according to the eternal religion and there will be peace and unity in the entire world. The Wheel of Time turns according to my wishes and this wish will soon take form.'

As foretold by Krishna, after some time Aurobindo and his companions were allowed to go free and Aurobindo's wisdom continues to inspire devotees who keep alive the true religion until the return of the Golden Age.

☆☆☆☆☆

Glossary

A

Adharma	Ungodly, Anti-dharma (irreligious), Shani
Adharma-Shani	Manifestation of the dark force under the influence of the Sun, Against the Gods, particularly Dharma, his step brother
Aditi	Mother of the Gods
Agni	God of Fire
Apsara	Dancing girl of heaven
Arbuda	Snake King
Arjun	The third Pandava, the intimate friend of Divine Krishna
Ashram	Place of religious study under the guidance of a guru
Astika	Son of Jaratkaru, Nephew of Vasuki
Asura	Undivine being, Titan, demon, hostile, opponent of the power of God
Avatar	Incarnation

B

Balrama	Brother of Krishna
Bhima	Second Pandava
Brahma	Creator of All
Brahman	The Supreme
Brihaspati	Teacher of the Gods

Devayana	The Third Epic of India, describes the Four Ages, together with the Movement of the Gods towards humanity and of humanity towards the Gods for the manifestation of the Golden Age.

D

Devi	Goddess
Dharma	Son of Surya (Sun) also known as Yama
Diti	Mother of the Asuras
Draupadi	Daughter of Drupad, wife of the Pandava brothers
Dwarka	Capital of Krishna's kingdom
Dwapara	Bronze Age

G

Ganapati	Son of Shiva
Ganesh	Another name of Ganapati
Gandharva	Demi-gods, celestial musician
Gathini	Daughter of Kushika, wife of Pragatha. Mother of Kali, Lord of the Iron Age
Guru	Spiritual Teacher

H

Himalaya	Biggest mountain range of India

I

Indra	The King of the Gods, Supreme Being

J

Janmejaya	Son of Parikshit

K

Kali	The Lord of the Iron Age, the Kali Yuga
Kali Yuga	Period of Time influenced by Kali
Krishna	Vishnu's incarnation during the Bronze Age
Kurukshetra	Battlefield of Kauravas and the Pandavas

M

Mahabharata	Second Epic of India
Mahakâla Pingala	A creative aspect of Shiva, a poetic form
Mahamâya	Great attachment, Durga, Maheshwari
Manasa	Mother of Rishi Astika, Jagatgauri

N

Naga	Snake

O

Om	The primal sound, Aksharabrahman

P

Pandavas	Sons of King Pandu, called the Pandavas – Yudhisthira, Bhima, Arjun, Nakul and Sahadeva
Pandavaya	Descendent of Pandavas – Parikshit, Janmejaya etc.
Parikshit	Grandson of Arjun
Pingal	The Poetic existence, the poetic form of Maheshwara
Pragatha	Son of Kanwa, father of Kali, the Lord of the Iron Age

R

Ramayana	First epic of India written by Valmiki Rishi-A Seer

S

Sanatana Dharma	Eternal religion
Satya	Truth
Satyadeva	Lord of Truth
Satya Yuga	Golden Age
Shani	Saturn
Shukracharya	Teacher of the Asuras
Snake	One with undivine power
Surya	Sun, Lord of Mental Truth

T

Takshaka	The snake who bit King Parikshit and killed him

Tapasya	Religious austerity, penance, discipline for the achievement of power
Tretayuga	Silver Age

V

Vasuki	The Snake King who holds the creation on his head in the subtle world
Vayu	Lord of the Wind, the Life Force, Commander of the Divine Forces
Vritra	The Leader of the Asuras, son of Diti
Vyadhi	Malady

Y

Yadavas	Krishna's family, clan
Yajna	A sacrifice, the flame of sacrifice
Yama	Eldest Son of Surya, the Sun
Yudhisthir	The eldest Pandava
Yuga	Age

☆☆☆☆☆

OTHER BOOKS BY AMITA NATHWANI

- Glimpses of Devayana
- The Voice of the Rsis
- Tales from the Devayana
- Devayan Vols. (I – X)

An epic always precedes the changing of an age in India. This is apparent from the past. Before the passage from the Silver to the Bronze Age, Ramayana was recorded. Mahabharata was written before the transition from the Bronze to the Iron Age. Now with the Iron Age coming to an end, and with the Golden Age approaching, a new epic, Devayan, has manifested.

Devayan, unlike the former two epics, does not only reveal to us the approaching Golden Age. Instead it describes the complete human cycle of 26,000 years covering the Golden, the Silver, the Bronze and the Iron Ages. It consists of twelve volumes, with a thousand pages each, divided into thirty-two books, written in the Anushthupa metre, the classical Indian epic metre. It deals with the "origin and the creation of the universe"; the complete history of the world during the Four Ages, including the approaching Golden Age. This is the age of the Supramental consciousness as envisaged by Sri Aurobindo. Man will evolve into a being with a totally new and divine consciousness based upon the Vedic truths. The great Indian tradition lives on.

The Black Princess
Maggie Voysey Paun
Pages : 326
Edition : Paperback
ISBN : 978-81-9363-136-2
Subject : Biographical Fiction

About the Book

Who is Mrs Helena Bennett and how did she come to live alone in the remote Sussex countryside?

Her neighbours know her as an eccentric old woman who roams the forest with her beloved dog, is generous to the poor, and smokes a hookah. They call her 'The Black Princess', although she is not very dark-skinned nor of Royal birth.

It is spring 1853 when a chance visitor causes Helena to begin to recall her early life. Through her eyes the reader is transported to 1785 at the British Residency in Lucknow, India, a city renowned for its hybrid culture, the excesses of the ruling Nawab, and the avarice of some of the East India Company officers.

The Black Princess is based on a true story.

Maggie Voysey Paun has published stories about Indian children living in England and has written plays and adult novels which all have some connection with India. She has been married for many years to Rashmi and they have three sons and five grandchildren.

Her previous novel Sacrifices which is set in Africa, was published in 2016 by PublishNation and is also available as an e-book or in paperback from Amazon.com.

Ninety Days Escape from Uganda
Rashmi Paun
Pages : 396
Edition : Paperback
ISBN : 978-81-9363-139-3
Subject : Biographical Fiction

About the Book

Ninety Days is a story about what life was like for Asians in Uganda before the President ordered them all to leave, and what happened afterwards as law and order broke down and people considered themselves lucky to escape unharmed.

In August 1972 President Idi Amin announced that God had come to him in a dream and told him to order citizens of Asian origin out of the country. He declared: 'If they are not out in Ninety days, they will soon see what happens to them!'

The story centres on the Hindu Mitani family whose biggest problems before the announcement are their elder son's choice of a Muslim wife, a sister's unhappy marriage and whether or not the community should spend its money on yet another religious shrine. But as the deadline approaches and there are beatings and imprisonments they, like their friends and neighbours, become increasingly desperate to find refuge in whichever country will take them, though they must flee more or less penniless and leave all their possessions behind.

Within ninety days, 70,000 members of what had been a close community many of whom were born in Uganda, were scattered across the world, mostly in the UK, Canada, India and the US, but some others across Europe and as far afield as Australia and New Zealand.

Rashmi Paun grew up in Jinja, Uganda. In 1972, when Amin made his announcement, Rashmi was already in London, studying for a doctorate in Physics, but his parents, family and friends were forced to flee from Amin's terror.